THE DO'S AND DON'TS OF DIVORCE

How to keep your sanity
Protect your children
& Live in peace

Dilyse Diaz, M.A., L.M.F.T.

ABOUT THE AUTHOR:

Dilyse Diaz is a Licensed Marriage and Family Therapist and is also a Special Master for the Los Angeles County Superior Court. As a Licensed Psychotherapist, Dilyse specializes in high conflict divorce and has helped many desperate families find hope and healing. With her skill, knowledge and expertise, Dilyse has had a thriving counseling private practice in Valencia, California for over 13 years. Dilyse is a parenting expert and incorporates many years of experience and wisdom into the application and content of this powerful book. Dilyse has successfully navigated the landmines of divorce and is raising her four happy children.

Please visit her website at www.DilyseDiazTherapy.com
Or Email her at Dilyse@DilyseDiazTherapy.com

CONTENTS

INTRODUCTION

Want to reduce the problems your child will go through after your divorce? Would practical skills to improve your life help you? You want your child to experience love, understanding and emotional safety throughout the divorce process, right? After all you have been through and are going through now, you may doubt it is possible to keep your sanity, protect your children and live in peace. The good news is that you can. It is not up to anyone else but you! YOU have the power to create a great outcome from a not-so-great situation. Let me teach you how...

I am so glad you decided to read this *quick, simple* and *powerful* book so that you can stabilize your sanity, which will protect your children. There is nothing more noble than doing the RIGHT thing for the sake of a child's emotional health and well-being. Follow the guidelines in this easy-to-read divorce manual and create peace, calm, love, encouragement, hopefulness and an opportunity for a second chance to do life BETTER!

You probably have heard by now that nearly 1 out of every 2 marriages ends in divorce. But, do you realize that children of divorce pay the highest price? The information outlined here is vital. You must know these things if you want to protect your children. I am confident that you, like everyone else, haven't been taught how to sanely go through a divorce. Chances are if you couldn't make the relationship work with your partner, you are even *more* unclear about how to divorce "well." I encourage you to take what *didn't* work in your life and use it as an opportunity to improve yourself. Here are new ways to shape your thoughts, feelings, behaviors and habits so you can be EFFECTIVE in every aspect of your life.

You are not alone. I will help you create a better future. When you enhance your coping skills, you are better equipped to deal with life. By increasing your knowledge, you amp up your power to create the life you want. I am here to help you choose better behaviors and make wiser decisions when it comes to the most critical job in life: parenting through a divorce. Parenting is hard enough, but if you add the dynamics of a divorce, you set yourself up for a potential disaster. It doesn't have to be. Help is here. *Your better life begins now.*

Change requires new actions. Keep these tips in mind as you read the "Do's" and "Don'ts" of Divorce:

- Stop for a moment and realize that a chaotic divorce can have long-lasting damaging effects. Acknowledge yourself for making changes by reading this book.

- Do one small, positive thing differently. It doesn't matter how small it is, just so long as you do SOMETHING different. This will start a chain reaction for more good things to come.

- Transform yourself. Be disciplined. Read all the tips in this tool-kit and follow the suggestions. Learn to handle *yourself* better, so that you will positively impact your child's experience of divorce. Tell yourself, **"Divorce doesn't have to be tragic."**

- Decide to change right now, this very moment! Commit yourself to doing everything in this manual to improve and help your family. Make a "direction correction" and forge a new path. Tell yourself, **"I can do this."**

- Empower and equip yourself with the tools you will learn in this book. There are many effective ways to handle your divorce. Learn and apply everything you possibly can!

- Get a journal or something to write your thoughts, feelings and goals down. Prepare yourself for a great, new life.

Wake up and pay attention.
Awareness is the gateway to change.

Do know that your child needs you to be healthy and strong.

Don't leave your children to handle their wounds without help and support.

"My mom and dad don't know that I cut myself. No one knows my secret pain inside. I feel alone and lost. I don't know what to do or how to get through this." **Sara, age 15**

Sara is not the only child who is silently suffering. I have been working with children of divorce for 15 years and my professional experience is that children have a lot going on deep inside that they don't dare share. They stuff it all down and feel alone, confused, angry, lost and ashamed. They need help navigating through their family's divorce. Please listen. Children are the helpless victims, not you! They are on the receiving end of parent's reactive, emotional and irrational behavior. *(Note: EVERYONE going through a divorce will, at some point, be reactive, emotional and irrational.)* Your job is to learn how to effectively manage these emotions. I am glad you are reading this manual to live differently.

I can tell you that your children don't know how to manage all the emotions going on inside. They need help. They didn't have a voice or choice in the decision to part ways. The world as they know it has been temporarily turned upside-down. Divorcing families become consumed with fighting about custody, child support and launching bombs of blame. Face it, neither parent wants to carry the guilt and wear the label as the one responsible for the divorce.

Children are stuck in the middle of parental combat. Adults don't realize that. Even if you think you would never put your child in the middle, you probably aren't aware that you do. I hear about it all the time in my private practice. You can prevent tragedies. Don't be blind to your child's suffering. Don't allow your own issues, pain and anger to cloud your vision of doing what is right. Children need to be seen *and* heard. They are often left behind with broken hearts, confusion and buried pain. The unaddressed hurt can be toxic. Find ways to open up, talk, share, comfort and support your child, so they can bring out what is buried deep inside. If they are left to interpret their experience on their own, they form mistaken beliefs. Some examples of these mistaken beliefs are:

"I am responsible for the divorce because all they fight about is me."

"I am never going to survive this. I feel so overwhelmed."

Children develop a depressed outlook that life is never going to get better. Heavy feelings of worry, guilt and pain weigh them down. Read this poem written by 18-year-old, Tyler. His words represent how many children of divorce feel.

I Don't Really Love Them

I am seventeen years old

My parents divorced when I was ten

People say I look fine

Well that's because I don't show it on the outside

I keep it all up inside

I'm angry at my parents

Because I think they love to argue and fight each other

More than they love me

I can always hear them arguing over the phone

They probably don't realize

That it's just hurting me more

Than it is helping

I love them because they are my family

But I don't really love them

It's been like this for seven years

Seven long years of hell

It's funny, I don't ever recall

When them loving me was more important than fighting each other

I have to love them because they are my family

But in truth

I don't love them at all.

"I wrote this poem from my own experience," Tyler said. "It tells a certain sadness of my life I have been struggling with for seven years. The poem reveals the feelings I have buried inside. This poem describes my feelings about my parents. I wished that things were different. There are certain things you cannot control. I wish things were different, but sometimes, you don't ever get your wish."

After discovering Tyler's poem, his parents took this as a wake-up call, heard his cry and listened. His parents finally recognized that their behaviors were harming him. Tyler did an incredible job of expressing all his buried feelings. His words are heart-breaking, shocking, eye-opening, powerful and real. Because he expressed himself, his parents are actively working together to build a positive relationship for their family.

We need to rescue our children now! It's time for you to get serious and attune to the inner world of your child, today, not seven years from now. Make life changes that will affect your family for generations to come. I applaud you for taking the time to read and apply the critical tasks you need to START and STOP doing right now! The aftermath of the emotionally (and sometimes physically) violent battle is too high a price to pay for any child. This burden is one that no child is meant to carry, but so many do. Don't let your child's suffering go unnoticed. If you sweep it all under the rug, things will begin to fester until their hidden pain evolves into a glaring crisis that is even more challenging than the original problem. Some examples of common red flags of a child attempting to cope with pain are: *isolation, defiance, dropping grades, acting out, using drugs, alcohol, sex, or cutting themselves.* Don't let things escalate to this point. I know you are someone who really understands this concept because you are NOT waiting another second of another day to change your life. Good for you!

What behaviors need your time and attention? Be honest. (i.e. I am worried about my son's dropping grades, my short temper and my daughter withdrawing from me.) Write your concerns for your family here:

_____

Acting out, withdrawing and isolation are ways your children communicate the message:

"I need HELP to cope with all of this mess! I am overwhelmed and don't know how to handle all of these heavy feelings!"

I am here to teach you how to help you and your children.

Here we go. This is going to be great!

CHAPTER 1

THE "DON'TS" OF DIVORCE

DON'T fight in front of the children.

"I cry in my pillow when I hear them yelling and arguing with each other. It's always something about me and I feel like it is all my fault. Maybe if I wasn't around, life would be better for them." **Joey, age 10**

Your children have experienced enough negativity. Stop engaging in the fighting. Leave the heavy discussions for when your children aren't around (actually, save it for when they are NOT HOME, not just in the other room). Children hear you, even when you think they can't. If you engage in a heated discussion, children feel fear and experience stress. When parents fight, it's terrifying for the kids. It changes who they are and it skews the person they are meant to become. They learn to handle conflict by watching how you handle problems. What are you currently teaching them? How will they learn to resolve problems based on watching you? Is there something you would change? Make your new focus *problem solving*, NOT winning the argument. Your children are uncomfortable when you fight and most likely won't want to be around you. Your hope is to grow closer to your child and create safety, so remember that fighting is not the path that will lead you to that goal. You can't control your ex, but you can change you.

<u>FACT:</u> The best way to change someone else's behavior is to first change your own.

Get ahold of your reactivity and do your own personal work to *respond* rather than *react* when your ex attempts to push your buttons. When you notice your buttons are pushed, DON'T react like a toy that lights up with bells and whistles going off when its buttons are pushed. Instead, be the "button" that doesn't work. They can push and push your "button" but they will begin to see that nothing is happening. You are not reacting. When she/he sees that these tactics aren't working, she/he will stop pushing the button. This method works. When you observe that your lack of reactivity changes the whole dynamic, I want to pause and realize that you made that happen because you chose to stop reacting. You empowered yourself and stopped the behavior. This is a basic, well-known principle. ***People only do what works. When it doesn't work anymore, they stop doing it.***

MY NEW COMMITMENT:

The change I am making now is _____

I am committed to making this change by doing these 3 things differently:

1.

2.

3.

**DON'T stop contact with your children...
EVER!**

*"When my dad divorced my mom, it was like he divorced
me, too. I guess there is something about me that he doesn't
like. I guess I am not worth his time. If I was good enough, he
would want to still see me."* **Carmen, age 13**

No matter what your reason or "excuse" may be, always invest in
fighting FOR your relationship with your child. Never give up on
them. EVER! They are NOT your ex. They deserve your love. They
need your influence in their life. When you allow your issues to
interfere with your relationship with your child, they will take it
personally and assume that there must be something damaged
or faulty about them. They grow up believing they are damaged.
Addictions, dysfunctional relationships, difficulty with intimacy
and other destructive patterns are often born from an absent parent. Children don't know how to interpret an absent parent cor-
rectly, so they will assume that if they were only "good enough,
pretty enough, smart enough or _____ enough," then their parent
would have stuck around. The reality is that this abandonment has
NOTHING to do with the child, and everything to do with the
parent lacking coping skills to know WHAT to do. Adults must
face their situation, fight for their child and do their own emotional
work to know how to separate the "adult stuff" from their relationship with their child they brought in to this world. There is no excuse, reason or rationalization that justifies not having, developing
and nurturing your relationship with your child. The court system
today is in total support of both parents having equal influence on
their children when they observe they are healthy and fit parents. If
you are doing your part in being the "healthy and fit" parent, then
there is no reason the courts will not support you having an equal
role in your child's life. If you don't have money for court, there are

many programs in place to help support you retaining an attorney so that you can have an active parenting role with your child. No excuses.

MY NEW COMMITMENT:

The change I am making now is _____

I am committed to making this change by doing these 3 things differently:

1.

2.

3.

DON'T put them in the middle... EVER!

"I feel so weird when my mom asks me about my dad's new girlfriend. I don't know what I am supposed to tell her. She gets mad if I don't tell her and she gets upset when I do tell her. I just want to run away. I don't want to hurt her feelings, but I don't want to tell her either. I wish she'd stop it."
Melanie, age 12

You put your child in the middle when you ask questions about the other parent or when you ask them to give information to the other parent. What the other parent does in the privacy of their new home is their business. All questions, concerns, inquiries or issues need to be made directly to the other parent and NEVER through your child.

NOTE: If your child is being emotionally, physically or sexually abused, you must immediately put a stop to it. Safety is always a reason to step in and protect them. If at any time you believe your child is being abused, call 911 or the Department of Children and Family Services immediately.

Another way parents put their children in the middle is when they use their children as a confidante and speak to them like they would a close friend. This robs children of their innocence. They don't need to feel burdened with adult business. That's way too much information for a child and their brains literally can't process adult matters. What ends up happening is the child misinterprets things, takes on a pseudo-adult role and they lose their innocence. They are not your equal. Children are NOT there to take care of you, listen to you, participate in adult matters or be a secret keeper to the adult's emotional world. If you use your child as a person you rely on for emotional support, you end up placing cruel expectations on that child to take care of you. That is not their job. They are there to be carefree children, not miniature adults, or new "best friend." Find another adult to help you process your emotions or seek professional guidance. You need support and direction too. Be sure to get it from an adult.

MY NEW COMMITMENT:

The change I am making now is _____

I am committed to making this change by doing these 3 things differently:

1.

2.

3.

DON'T use them as messengers between you and the other parent.

"Daddy would always say, 'Tell your mom she owes me money for your hair.' I always hated that and felt like I was in the middle. I was made to be the adult in the situation and I thought my dad should be the adult, not me. It's his money that she owes and it sucks to be in the middle of all that." **Meghin, age 16**

No child should be made to do the adult's job. EVER. Take the burden off your child and figure out an appropriate way to communicate with the other parent. There are current resources available to you, like the computer program called "The Family Wizard" that will help monitor your communication if that is a source of difficulty for you. Directly communicate with the other parent when you need something done.

MY NEW COMMITMENT:

The change I am making now is _____

I am committed to making this change by doing these 3 things differently:

1.

2.

3.

DON'T make birthdays all about you!

"Yell, yell, yell! That is what my parents do on my birthday. I get "even years" with mom and "odd years" with dad. Seriously? I can't see my mom this year on my birthday? Whatever. I don't even want to celebrate. It has become the worst day of the year for me and it's supposed to be my special day. There isn't anything special about it now." **Philip, age 13**

Parents, please find a way to get over yourselves and see the day from your child's perspective. It is not about you. Birthdays aren't about your fight, your divorce or how much you hate the other person; it's about celebrating the life of your wonderful child who you made together. Find a way to put aside your differences. Ultimately, if you would be willing to swallow your pride, ego and self-centeredness and have a joint birthday party or go to dinner together with your child and act kindly, your child would really enjoy that. I know you may think that is crazy now, but plant that seed and grow into the ability to celebrate your child's life together. Make it a day your child wants to celebrate again.

MY NEW COMMITMENT:

The change I am making now is _____

I am committed to making this change by doing these 3 things differently:

1.

2.

3.

DON'T make them choose sides or loyalties.

"Looking back at the time they said they were getting a divorce, my dad really did paint my mom out to be a crazy person. He did that so I would always choose to be with him, (which at that time, I did). I started being a totally mean person to my mom and refused to go to her house after the divorce. Now that I am older, I suffer from horrible guilt about how I treated her. My mom is a really loving person and I see that now. I couldn't see it at first because of how my dad painted such a horrible picture of her and told me things that I had no business being a part of. I wish I would have known better back then. I feel so depressed now. I question myself all the time. How could I have been so horrible to her? I have a lot of anger towards my dad now that I see that he really set me up to choose sides." **Marilyn, age 18**

This is the single most damaging event to a child's psyche. Making your child choose a position against the other parent is *cruel.* Don't put pressure on them or manipulate them about where they want to live. They need to feel you support their relationship with the other parent. The fact is your child is made up of both you and their other parent. No matter what has happened, they will have an intrinsic loyalty to both of you.

MY NEW COMMITMENT:

The change I am making now is _____

I am committed to making this change by doing these 3 things differently:

1.

2.

3.

> **DON'T ask your child who they want to live with or what schedule they want.**

"The guilt I feel for choosing to be at my mom's for Christmas is overwhelming to me. But, that is where I wanted to be because my cousins are there. I wish they would just agree and not put me in the middle and ask me. Can't they work out the schedule for me to be with the cousins at Christmas so I don't have to feel like crap choosing one parent over the other?" **Jaclyn, age 17**

Making decisions about holiday times and living arrangements needs to be kept between the parents. Once you both decide how it is going to be, then tell your child his or her schedule with confidence, clarity and support in your tone of voice. *If your tone indicates or conveys disapproval or anger, then your child will most likely feel torn, guilty, hurt and angry.* You don't want them to feel those things unnecessarily, so don't make them choose a loyalty of one parent over the other. Do whatever it takes to discuss and agree (between the adults) upon a schedule while taking your child's needs and wants into consideration.

MY NEW COMMITMENT:

The change I am making now is _____

I am committed to making this change by doing these 3 things differently:

1.

2.

3.

DON'T give your support check to your child to give to your former spouse.

"I hate when my dad asks me to give my mom the child support check. I feel like I will be in trouble if I tell him no, and my stomach always gets in knots because my mom always seems mad about it when I give it to her. I hate feeling like this." **Bobby, age 9**

Don't involve your children in money matters! Don't ask them to deliver a support check or to get a support check from the other parent. Don't ever ask them to do the adult job of giving or receiving child support. If receiving or giving the child support check is at all problematic or difficult for you, then use the government service of your local Child Support Services office in your home town. They can set up to give, receive or garnish pay checks so child support checks can be given and received in a timely manner.

MY NEW COMMITMENT:

The change I am making now is _____

I am committed to making this change by doing these 3 things differently:

1.

2.

3.

DON'T belittle or talk negatively about the other spouse.

"Even when my dad 'jokingly' calls my mom names or is 'playfully' sarcastic about how she does something, I know he is putting her down and it is mean. I don't like it. I feel bad that he is passively mean to her. I am like her in those ways, so it just makes me feel like he doesn't really like me either. It makes me sad." **Jenna, age 12**

Your child is made from the other parent too and believe it or not, they will interpret and take on your criticism of that parent. When your kids internalize your criticism, the message to them is that they are "bad" or not liked by you. That is an awful message to pass on to your child. Be sensitive about how you talk about the other parent. Even if you think you are being sly by masking your anger or hatred in sarcasm or playful banter, children can see right through that and take it personally against their own character. Instead of being directly rude or passively sarcastic, go out of your way to say something truly complimentary about the other parent for your child's sake.

MY NEW COMMITMENT:

The change I am making now is _____

I am committed to making this change by doing these 3 things differently:

1.

2.

3.

DON'T allow your resentment or bitterness toward your ex to spill over into your relationship with your children.

"After my dad gets off the phone with my mom, he is in a really bad mood. He snaps and yells at me and punishes me for no reason. I know he is mad at her, but why does he have to take it out on me?" **Michael, age 8**

Staying mad, bitter or angry at the other parent takes away from your beautiful relationship you could have with your child. Tension in the home is toxic. With the additional conflict, the message children develop is that "home" is no longer their safe haven. We want them to feel good, safe and loved at home. We want them to *want* to be at home. Take the energy you spend being angry and invest that same effort into developing an amazing, healthy relationship with your child. Stop giving your power away to the other parent. When you allow them to affect who you are and how you behave, you give them permission to define you. This is what I mean when I say you give your power away to the other parent. No matter what they say, how they say it, or what they believe, **it doesn't make it true. YOU define YOU.** Start investing time, money, energy and effort into your relationships, your home life, your family and your world and stop caring about what the other parent thinks, says, believes or does.

MY NEW COMMITMENT:

The change I am making now is _____

I am committed to making this change by doing these 3 things differently:

1.

2.

3.

> **DON'T shut down your child down from talking about the divorce.**

"My dad and my mom snap at me when I ask anything about the divorce. I have no one to talk to and I am really confused. All these bottled up emotions get me super depressed." **Scott, age 13**

Your children have their own thoughts, questions and opinions about the divorce and they are *theirs* and they are *valid*. If you don't know what to say, here is something you can validate them with while not having to know all the answers:

"I really see how upset you are by all of this. I am here for you and love you. I don't know all the answers right now, but I promise you, we will figure this out and you WILL be okay."

MY NEW COMMITMENT:

The change I am making now is _____

I am committed to making this change by doing these 3 things differently:

1.

2.

3.

DON'T let your guilt stop you from disciplining appropriately.

"Now that my parents are divorced, I don't have any rules. I stay out as late as I want and no one tells me no. I feel like no one cares about me anymore." **Maggie, age 13**

Boundaries, limits, rules and discipline equal SAFETY AND LOVE. Learn effective parenting and proper limit setting to grow a happy, healthy, secure child. Letting your child "off the hook" from consequences isn't a loving, kind, nurturing thing to do at all. Children grow up and learn through experiences that they are bound to certain rules of society. When they don't know how to follow rules or accept "no" as an answer, they end up getting in trouble and may have a much higher price to pay later. Teach them now how to accept "no" for an answer, along with the truth that *every choice they make comes with a consequence*. Good choices breed good outcomes. Bad choices bring unpleasant consequences. You are their guide. Discipline them in a loving, firm and clear way. When you are consistent and take time to show you care by having rules and following through with consequences, your children will less likely experience social and emotional problems. Being emotionally available with your child helps them handle their own emotions better. When you are consistent with discipline, you calm your environment and create peace.

MY NEW COMMITMENT:

The change I am making now is _____

I am committed to making this change by doing these 3 things differently:

1.

2.

3.

DON'T buy their love.

"My mom is always working. My dad is always working. On the weekends, they are off doing their own thing. They buy me things all the time. They think that is love? I would give anything just to have them take a minute and look me in the eyes and ask me how I am doing." **Amanda, age 12**

Your children want you to be available to spend time with them and build a relationship that feels complete and safe. Buying, spoiling or indulging them with "things" won't fill them up in the long run. Your time, attention and interest in them will be what will shape them into healthy, well-adjusted adults later. Gifts and things to overcompensate for your guilt about being divorced is not the approach to take. Plan an activity today and go do it. Warning: they may be uncomfortable at first, but hang in there and do it anyway. Make this a new habit. Soon, you will reap the benefits of a happy and fulfilling relationship with the investment of your time, love and energy.

MY NEW COMMITMENT:

The change I am making now is _____

I am committed to making this change by doing these 3 things differently:

1.

2.

3.

DON'T try to control the parenting methods of the other parent.

"My dad tries to control my mom. My mom tries to change my dad. GEEZ! Get over it. I can't stand either of them when all they do is argue. They are divorced and they are still fighting over the stupidest things! They wonder why I'm always out with friends. All they both do is think of themselves without ever thinking about how they affect me and my brothers." **Bobby, age 18**

It is wonderful if you can be on the same page or even in the same book as the other parent, but many times, that isn't possible. You can't control other people. If your ex isn't willing to co-parent with you, then let it go. Let your child and their other parent's relationship develop as their relationship. Don't interfere. Encourage communication. Inspire them to work on it. Beyond that, let it go.

MY NEW COMMITMENT:

The change I am making now is _____

I am committed to making this change by doing these 3 things differently:

1.

2.

3.

> **DON'T fail to take care of your child's needs just because you are mad at the other parent.**

"My dad wouldn't pick me up when my mom was working and going to be late. He said, 'It's her day, so she needs to do it.' I was stuck at school for an extra hour and felt pretty abandoned by both of them." **Jared, age 14**

Kids always pay the price. Do what you need to do. Help, even if it is "the other parent's day." When you are helping your child, you are telling them you value you them, no matter what anyone else chooses to do. The kids come first. If you can help, then do what it takes. Take the high road and be there for your child.

MY NEW COMMITMENT:

The change I am making now is _____

I am committed to making this change by doing these 3 things differently:

1.

2.

3.

DON'T undermine the other parent, no matter how you feel.

"My mom says there is a court order that I can only talk to my dad at certain times. I miss him and don't understand why I can't talk to him whenever I want. At my dad's, I can call my mom whenever I feel like it. I don't understand."
Selena, age 6

There are obvious ways to undermine the other parent. "Your mom is a cheater" or "Your dad is a selfish jerk." But, there are more subtle ways that adults undermine each other when it comes to post divorce co-parenting. Laying a guilt trip on a child who wants to talk to their other parent is a move that undermines that child's bond and relationship with the other parent. Telling the child how miserable you will be without them and how you will be so sad while they are gone is another awful undermining move. You basically are saying, *"I am not happy unless you are with me, so make sure you aren't having a good time when you are with your dad/mom."* You set that child and other parent up for a miserable time together (which is undermining them!). If the child enjoys themselves, you have now saddled them with guilt and responsibility for your happiness or sadness. AWFUL! Be a responsible parent. Encourage them to speak to their other parent by phone without having to get a court order for managing phone calls. Encourage them (out loud) to have a great time whenever they are with their other parent.

MY NEW COMMITMENT:

The change I am making now is _____

I am committed to making this change by doing these 3 things differently:

1.

2.

3.

DON'T manipulate or emotionally blackmail your child.

"Being used for a personal vendetta by my mom crushed me. I will never be able to fully recover from the heart-wrenching trauma I was put through. I am successful in spite of her, not at all because of her." **Lila, age 18**

When you coerce or manipulate your child, you are basically saying, *"I'm cutting you off or not giving you something so I can manipulate you into giving me what I want."* Your child will end up resenting you. It is an awful way function in a relationship with anyone, especially your child. You will end up isolating yourself from your child. For example, when you threaten your teen with not allowing them to get a driver's license if they don't live with you, or do what you want regarding the divorce, you are using them in a very harmful way. I believe this is one of the worst forms of abuse because it is so subtle. Manipulating, withholding love, preventing them from getting something important to them, threatening to not pay for college if they don't do what you want is punitive, cruel and the epitome of narcissism. This type of coercive control will only drive you apart from your child. Put your feelings for your ex and yourself aside and focus on the real priority, which is a healthy, loving, attuned relationship with your child.

MY NEW COMMITMENT:

The change I am making now is _____

I am committed to making this change by doing these 3 things differently:

1.

2.

3.

DON'T use your children for YOUR emotional support or comfort.

"When I was a little girl, my mom and dad would viciously fight and my mom would run away from her problems and "escape" for an entire weekend, whisking me away with her. I was her comforter. I was four. Looking back, I realize that all of my childhood was spent carrying the emotional burden of being responsible for her – her feelings, happiness, sadness, and misery. I felt good if she was happy, and unbearably sad when she was unhappy. My mom was most often unhappy. Everything revolved around her. I was invisible. I don't remember a time when she stopped and looked me in the eyes and asked about me, my feelings or my life. When I became a teenager, I could never figure out why I didn't matter enough for her to take an interest in my life and hobbies. I formed a belief at a very young age that I was only valuable when I took care of others. When they were happy with me, I felt happy. If they thought negatively of me, I was devastated and questioned the worthiness of my existence. I learned to define myself by what everyone else thought of me. What a roller coaster ride. I was like a yo-yo of everyone else's definition of what they thought of me. It was exhausting and a powerless, hopeless place. For a long time, even a great deal of my adult life, I dismissed my own feelings in order to take care of other people's. I knew life could be better, but I just didn't know how. I spent many years educating myself so that I can create a different life--a better life. My personal journey has been long, amazing, pain-staking, awakening, challenging, exciting and very worthwhile. I have used every experience as an opportunity to grow. I am grateful for the mentors that helped me become the strong, successful woman I am today. Each difficulty has been an important

piece to my incredible puzzle of self-discovery and personal growth. Because I have chosen to be vulnerable and bravely take this journey of self-discovery, I succeed today." **Dilyse Diaz, L.M.F.T. (Author)**

Parents have a powerful influence. Adults, rightly so, have needs and deserve comfort and emotional support, but not from their children. Divorce is a horrible time of heavy loss, but the children should NEVER, EVER be used as an emotional crutch. They are not responsible for making you feel better. You are responsible for making you feel better. It is grossly inappropriate to say your child is "your best friend," or "he/she is there for me like no one else." Learn to manage your own feelings. Your child is not tied to or responsible for your emotional stability. When you rely on your child for comfort, you use them up for your own satisfaction. They need to be kids. You need to be there for them, not the other way around. You are the adult. They are growing, needy children. They need you to take care of them. Take care of your own emotional burdens so that you can see them, hear them and value them for who they are as unique, special, important and SEPARATE individuals. If they are always taking care of you, they fail to learn how to care of themselves. This backwards way of parenting creates dysfunction in children's lives and leaves them vulnerable to really dysfunctional relationships later in life. Find another adult friend, support group or personal therapist to help you. You deserve love and support; get it from another adult.

MY NEW COMMITMENT:

The change I am making now is _____

I am committed to making this change by doing these 3 things differently:

1.

2.

3.

DON'T make your child the "man of the house" or "new mom" of the house.

"I feel so out of control when my little sister acts up. I am only 11 and she is 3. I don't know how to be a mom to her. She doesn't listen, so I yell at her and she cries and it's terrible. I am alone in taking care of her and my homework until my mom gets home at 6 p.m. I am really afraid something bad is going to happen and then I will really be in trouble." **Jackie, age 11**

Adults are in charge of running a home, not the children. Hire help or get an adult caregiver. Ask for help from friends. Do whatever you need to do to avoid putting children in charge of adult responsibilities. There is no way they can follow through like an adult because their brain is not developed to have the coping skills or problem solving abilities of an adult. They will inevitably mess up and then form the mistaken belief that they are somehow "screw-ups" for not doing it right. That is not kind, nor fair for them to be set up to fail. Kids need to be kids. What is stopping you from asking for help? Prioritize your children's mental health and well-being and make the necessary changes so your child is not burdened with the impression they are responsible to be the "head of the household."

MY NEW COMMITMENT:

The change I am making now is _____

I am committed to making this change by doing these 3 things differently:

1.

2.

3.

DON'T compare your child's negative behaviors to your ex-spouse

"My mom tells me 'you are just like your father.' Well, my dad is in jail for domestic violence, so I guess that means I am bad like him. I feel like hitting her when she tells me that." **Joseph, age 16**

Your children are individuals. Treat them like one. It doesn't matter if they have traits like their parent (of course they will), just don't use that to manipulate, shame, degrade or put them down. If you ever compare them to your ex, make it something that is wonderful, strong, amazing and complimentary about their other parent.

MY NEW COMMITMENT:

The change I am making now is _____

I am committed to making this change by doing these 3 things differently:

1.

2.

3.

DON'T belittle your child for struggling or acting out.

"My dad called me an f—ing baby when I got upset and started crying about not being able to do an Easter egg hunt. Because he belittled me about feeling sad, I vowed never to show my true emotion ever again." **Bobby, at age 10 (now 17)**

Your child is struggling to grow up and navigate the world of emotions, which is difficult enough, but when you add the difficulties of divorce into the mix, your child will most likely be more emotional than if they weren't going through all of this. Divorce has rocked their world, and they need extra compassion and understanding. Putting your child down because they are feeling sad, angry, emotional, etc. isn't the way to approach the problem. Put yourself in their shoes and seek a solution that is productive. Vow to never call them names under any circumstances and for any reason. EVER.

MY NEW COMMITMENT:

The change I am making now is _____

I am committed to making this change by doing these 3 things differently:

1.

2.

3.

DON'T introduce your child to your new boyfriend/girlfriend right away and when you do, don't be physically affectionate in front of your child until they are really comfortable with having a new adult in your life.

"My dad brought home Angela and I was not happy. They were always like teenagers when they were together. Finally, when I started liking her, they broke up. Then, he met Maggie. I refused to get close to her, but they were together for 8 months and I figured she was staying. I opened up to her and let her in, but then he broke up with her. Now, I just do my own thing and don't even talk to the new girlfriend." **Max, age 16**

If you are going to date, don't bring them home to meet your kids right away. If you are dating this person for more than four months and you believe that it is going well, then introduce them after that four-month mark as a friend. They don't need to see you both being physically affectionate with each other. It is as if you are shoving a reality they don't want down their throat. Emotionally, they are probably not ready to see another partner in your life. Tune in to how they feel and what they are saying how they feel about someone new in your life. Respect their feelings. If this new person is indeed sticking around, then there should be time to slowly get them used to the idea in a way that works for everyone.

MY NEW COMMITMENT:

The change I am making now is _____

I am committed to making this change by doing these 3 things differently:

1.

2.

3.

DON'T EVER GIVE UP.

"My mom has done everything in her power to be here for me. I know that even when my dad's a jerk or doesn't pay for things, she will. She listens, she cares, she takes me to a good therapist. I like my life and have gotten through all the hard stuff because she never gave up. She told me we would figure all the bad stuff out. She hugged me when I would cry. She let me be me, no matter how I felt. I learned that life did get better. Now, I know to never give up when other hard times come." **Denise, age 17**

Never give up. Never, ever give up on your hopes, goals, dreams and passion for life. If you or your child is struggling, know that things will get better if you invest in yourself. Figure out a great system to improve your life. Focus on the things that matter: yourself, your child, your family's well-being. You don't need to travel this journey alone and neither does your child. Get the help for you so you can help your child. There is nothing more secure than knowing that no matter what struggles are going on in your life, you will ALWAYS figure it out. At the end of the day, if you know you will always figure it out, you will always be okay. Anxiety, depression and other mental health issues come from the belief that you won't be okay. Create a new reality for yourself and your child and always learn to instill belief in them and say, ***"You will figure this out. You will always be ok. I am here to be by your side along the way."***

MY NEW COMMITMENT:

The change I am making now is _____

I am committed to making this change by doing these 3 things differently:

1.

2.

3.

CHAPTER 2

THE "DO'S" OF DIVORCE

DO notice, acknowledge, and support your children's thoughts, feelings and emotions.

"My mom and dad are out of control. They don't even notice that I am around. The only time I get any attention is when I am in trouble at school." **Katie, age 14**

If the only time your children get your full attention is when they are in trouble, then they will increase the time they are in trouble. Children don't have the ability to articulate their feelings and pain in an adult manner. Their brain development simply isn't there at this point. The way children sometimes tell you how they are hurting is by acting out their feelings of pain, confusion and loss. They can also withdraw and suddenly "disappear" without ever being noticed. These kids slip through the cracks and suffer in silence. *PAY ATTENTION TO ANY CHANGES IN THEIR BEHAVIOR.* When children disconnect from friends, family or life, they need your help. This withdrawal from life is your child telling you that they are struggling. In addition to the obvious cries for help, buried pain often comes out in some not so obvious forms. When a child suddenly becomes "annoying", difficult, or regresses through tantrums, they are telling you that they don't know how to manage all that they are feeling and experiencing inside. Parents can be caught up in their own problems and neglect to notice how much their children are suffering. Pay attention to the "misbehavior" and realize they are telling you:

"I need help managing my emotions."

If you don't know what to do or say, get them help with someone who can teach you how. Do act on what you see and avoid allowing things to get unmanageable or unbearable.

MY NEW COMMITMENT:

The change I am making now is _____

I am committed to making this change by doing these 3 things differently:

1.

2.

3.

DO know that your children are affected by YOUR issues. Deal with YOUR problems so your children NEVER have to take care of your problems and feelings. You are the adult and children are NEVER responsible for the adult.

"All my mom does is cry. I feel helpless. I wish I didn't have to hear her crying all the time. I try to comfort her but nothing helps. I feel useless." **Jennifer, age 11**

It is critical for you to get help, so that you are emotionally available to help your children. If you are upset with the other parent, you can sometimes overlook your child. When you are so consumed by all the "junk" from your divorce, your children feel dismissed or "shooed away." Divorce is overwhelming. Take care of yourself so you can take care of your child. They need you to be healthy and happy, so that they can be healthy, happy and emotionally stable. Many dysfunctional issues arise when a child has to be the emotional and/or the physical caretaker of an adult. It is NOT a child's job to take care of their parent. You deserve to invest time, money, and energy in yourself. Start now. What is one thing you can do for *you* today?

MY NEW COMMITMENT:

The change I am making now is _____

I am committed to making this change by doing these 3 things differently:

1.

2.

3.

> **DO make time for each child individually and LISTEN reflectively to what is going on in THEIR world.**

"My favorite thing to do, even with all the bad stuff going on, is to play a card game with my dad. I know he is so busy, but when he and I play together, I feel like I matter." **Joey, age 14**

Stop for 10 minutes. We all have busy schedules and many things that take up our time, but we can make a window of undivided attention for 10 minutes. Make this a priority.

- Take your children somewhere away from the house to spend time just with them.

- Ask them open-ended questions like, **"What was the best part of your day?"**

- Listen without commentary or judgment. Reflective listening basically means that you repeat back to them the things you hear them saying to you.

- Inquire about their hobbies and interests. Reflect back what you are hearing.

- Get to know them in a new way.

Show them that they matter. Make time each day to stop, look them in the eyes and be interested in what they have to say, no matter what it is.

MY NEW COMMITMENT:

The change I am making now is _____

I am committed to making this change by doing these 3 things differently:

1.

2.

3.

DO pay attention to your tone of voice and body language.

"Even though my mom says she is not mad, I can tell by the way she scrunches her eyebrows and squeezes her lips together that she is lying." **Carlton, age 9**

Have you been paying attention to the way you have been speaking or the way you come across with your body language lately? Listen to yourself. Watch yourself. What would someone think if they listened in on a conversation with you and your child or watched a video tape of you interacting with them? What would they see? Would they get the impression that you are a genuinely interested parent? Would they hear traces of anger in the way you speak? Would they get the impression that you are depressed, mad or anxious? People interpret what you are communicating more by your body language and tone of voice than the actual words coming out of your mouth. Body language and tone of voice speak louder than your words. In fact, 96% of what children take in comes from your non-verbal communication. Your stance, tone and eye contact (or lack thereof) speak the loudest. Do pay attention and be mindful of your true communication with your body language and tone of voice.

MY NEW COMMITMENT:

The change I am making now is _____

I am committed to making this change by doing these 3 things differently:

1.

2.

3.

> **DO have patience and read between the lines.**

"I was really surprised that my dad didn't flip out when I was being a real brat. He sat down, looked at me and told me that he noticed I was angry and asked me if I wanted to talk about it. I couldn't believe it. I felt really bad inside for being so bratty. But, I also felt really loved and cared about. I know I can turn to my dad now and I trust that he loves me for me, even when I mess up." **Samantha, age 17**

Reading between the lines means that instead of getting mad, reacting, yelling or lecturing your children for their misbehavior, you stay calm and ask yourself, ***"What might be going on for them?"*** Then, you address what you suspect may be happening for them. Use this new approach. When they slam a door out of anger, check your reactions and instead of yelling, say,

> *"I notice that you seem really angry right now. I am sorry you are having a hard time. This must be difficult for you. I can see that. I want you to know that I am here and available to help you when you want to talk about what is going on."*

Having patience and not taking their reactivity personally will enable you to respond calmly and actually help them. You have the power to turn the potentially volatile situation around. Respond patiently and lovingly. This will de-escalate the situation and help your child feel noticed, heard and loved. They are kids. They don't know how to manage all of these feelings until you teach them how.

MY NEW COMMITMENT:

The change I am making now is _____

I am committed to making this change by doing these 3 things differently:

1.

2.

3.

> **DO make sure they know they have your permission and blessing to love the other parent.**

"I know deep down that my mom will be hurt if I like being at my dad's house so I always come home and tell her all the bad things that happened there, even though I really did have a good time. I know she will feel better then."
Tom, age 13

What an awful thing for your child to believe that if they have a good time while they are not with you, then you will be upset! Make it clear to them (in your own words and actions) that you LOVE that they are happy when they are apart from you. Tell them that your heart would feel bad if they weren't having a good time. Clear up the terrible message or fear they might have that they shouldn't like the other parent or the idea that you would feel bad if they have fun with them. That is a burden you DON'T want them carrying! *They need to understand with their heart, mind, body and soul that they have your blessing and permission to love the other parent.* Even if you say you want them to have fun, ask yourself if your body language and tone of voice are in alignment with your words. If they get the message from you that it is not okay to like the other parent, or to have fun at their house, then you are taking away their ability to enjoy their company. Set them free and let them feel good about liking, loving and having fun with the other parent.

MY NEW COMMITMENT:

The change I am making now is _____

I am committed to making this change by doing these 3 things differently:

1.

2.

3.

> **DO learn to respect and support the other parent, regardless of how you feel now.**

"I actually feel better knowing I can't manipulate my mom when I am with my dad. I used to tell my mom one thing and my dad another to get what I wanted. At first, they fell for it and would fight, and I would get my way, but then they started catching on. Now, they talk first before believing the story I tell them. They actually back each other up. Even though I don't get my way, I feel better. I feel safe and not so out of control. I like that they can talk to each other now. I feel relieved when I don't have to worry about them hating each other." **Jimmy, age 14**

It is important that your children respect both parents. Believe me, they won't if they witness you degrading or disrespecting the other parent. Undermining the parent creates chaos in your child's mind. When children have too much power, they can feel out of control. They are not designed to rule the house and dictate or manipulate how things are to be. Even though you may not respect the other parent (you are, after all, getting a divorce), this is a new day and you are making the right choices because it is the right thing to do. You are heading down a new road. Strive for the greater good of your child. Be respectful, or at least cordial, and this will help your children. That may be hard, initially, but remember the reasons you chose to marry them. Jog your memory about what you once respected about your ex. What good things did you like? You are now in a position to evolve and treat your ex in a respectful way. You aren't living with them anymore. Find happiness in that! Just know that the few minutes you interact with them can be in your control. Make it a positive experience for your child. This really does benefit you AND your children, no matter how you feel about the other person.

FACT: **When you disrespect someone else, you are really disrespecting yourself.**

You want to be a calm and respectful person, correct? Don't give the other parent the power to change who you are.

FACT: **What you permit is what you teach.**

If you demonstrate disrespect, you teach your child to disrespect their parent and other authority figures in their lives. This is a really important point. Be respectful to your child's other parent. That lesson goes a <u>long</u> way.

MY NEW COMMITMENT:

The change I am making now is _____

I am committed to making this change by doing these 3 things differently:

1.

2.

3.

DO keep change to a minimum.

"I hate my life. I am bounced around ALL the time. There is no schedule at my dad's. Then, I go to my mom's and she is always changing things in my day. I never know what is happening. I am so confused! My grades are starting to drop and I can't keep track of anything in my life! I hate this stupid way of living! Oh, and then they send me to a doctor and label me as A.D.H.D! Don't they get it? I can't concentrate with all this stuff going on!" **Lenny, age 15**

Consistent schedules are CRITICAL in the midst of all the chaos. Schedules create predictability and predictability creates stability. Routine is beneficial to your whole family. Chances are, if you create a routine, you and your family will feel better and therefore, function better. If children feel better at home, they can focus better at school.

MY NEW COMMITMENT:

The change I am making now is _____

I am committed to making this change by doing these 3 things differently:

1.

2.

3.

DO continue to set boundaries and rules.

"I get away with everything now. I totally know how to play the guilt card on my parents. I do kinda feel bad but it's their problem to deal with it. I get so much more stuff now and I get away with a lot. I know how to work them."
Savannah, age 13

Sometimes, your guilt softens your discipline. Although children may feel they are getting more, they are getting less. They are learning a really bad pattern in their life to manipulate people into getting their way. This builds their sense of entitlement. Stop. Be clear about what your rules and boundaries are and KEEP them in place. Consistency builds stability. You don't want to add more difficulty to your child's already challenging experience. The reality is that a child's life is WORSE later if you don't discipline and follow through with your consequences NOW!

MY NEW COMMITMENT:

The change I am making now is _____

I am committed to making this change by doing these 3 things differently:

1.

2.

3.

DO continue to show your child you are not going away, no matter what.

"When my mom and dad divorced, my dad just stopped being a dad. He stopped coming over. He doesn't call me. He has a different life now with his new girlfriend. I worry a lot that my mom is going to do the same thing. That is why I get so angry when she goes out." **Jimmy, age 15**

This is one of the most important points. During a divorce, children are more susceptible to feeling abandoned. Show them with your ACTIONS that you aren't going anywhere and that you are there to care for them mentally, physically, emotionally and spiritually. If a parent puts other things and people in front of the child, she/he may feel neglected. Be cautious about dating or going out with friends before spending quality time with your children. Be there emotionally, mentally and physically. *If you aren't there for your child, they WILL find someone or something to fill the void.* Teens often turn to the wrong crowd, sex, drugs, alcohol, etc. You can certainly decrease the odds of future "daddy issues" or drug addiction by being a "present" parent. Being present means that you acknowledge, attune, notice and pay attention to what is happening right in front of you. With this present awareness, you can make yourself emotionally available. When a parent is physically and emotionally present with their child, trust is established. With trust, they know in their soul that you care, they matter, and you are always there for them. You are NEVER going away. You need to be their rock. Show them they are important and communicate that there is nothing they could do or say that would make you go away. You will love them even if they have negative feelings, or if they do something wrong. Does your child get the message that there is nothing they could do that would make you love them any less?

MY NEW COMMITMENT:

The change I am making now is _____

I am committed to making this change by doing these 3 things differently:

1.

2.

3.

DO create consistency in your home.

"My mom always says we are going to do something and then she changes her mind. She has excuses for everything. I get so angry inside. I don't trust her or anyone else anymore!" **Jeremiah, age 10**

Keep your agreements, commitments and promises. Mean what you say and say what you mean. Plan ahead. Develop structure. Have a bedtime. All of these routine things have to do with consistency. Consistency creates predictability, which promotes stability. Only make commitments and promises that you KNOW you can keep. If you aren't sure you can keep an agreement, but really want to do something for your child, say:

"You are important to me and I want to take you where you want to go, but I am not sure if I will have enough time today because I have already committed myself to something else. I know I can do it tomorrow for sure if today doesn't work out."

Children of divorce have had enough hardship and disappointment. Be consistent. Be clear. Be a parent they can count on.

MY NEW COMMITMENT:

The change I am making now is _____

I am committed to making this change by doing these 3 things differently:

1.

2.

3.

DO accept your child's opinions, even when they are different from yours.

"I love how I can be myself around my mom. I know that I don't have to say things just to please her or that she won't be mad if I don't agree with her. She has taught me to value others by accepting them when they have a different opinion than me. I learned that not everyone is going to agree with me and that when they don't, I still feel calm and worthy. We all can exist together with our own ideas. No one is right and no one is wrong. Because she listens and encourages me to express my own ideas, I know I matter and other people are important too." **Jenna, age 18**

People, all people, have a right to their opinion. Just because someone has an opinion, doesn't mean you have to adopt their opinion. It is important that you listen to their perspective, and just because you listen, doesn't mean you have to change your position. When you take time to listen, you are showing them they are valued. You can have different opinions and that is okay. You don't have to force your feelings on them, nor do you have to adopt their beliefs. Be open to listening to their perspective and take interest in what they have to say. Listen to their opinion without interjecting your own; this will set them up to learn how to be a separate self and an independent thinker. Being a whole, separate, worthy self is one of the most valuable qualities a person can develop. Remember, just because they have an opinion and you listen and value their opinion, doesn't mean you have to give in to it.

MY NEW COMMITMENT:

The change I am making now is _____

I am committed to making this change by doing these 3 things differently:

1.

2.

3.

DO get yourself into a grief/divorce support group to deal with your loss.

"My mom put me in a group with some new friends and I didn't even know what divorce meant! I didn't think ANYONE else knew what I was feeling or going through. Now, I have met a LOT of people who really understand me, even a girl from my school! The group really helped me and I feel so much happier." **Makenzie, age 6**

Divorce is a loss. It is like a death. It is a loss of a dream, a hope and a vision of how you thought things were going to be. This loss is serious and needs to be honored. Dealing with a heavy loss shouldn't be done alone or in isolation. You need support, love and care while coping with your loss. Seek support as soon as you detect difficulties in handling or helping your children. Waiting to deal with your problems only makes things worse. Get together with people who are going through something similar. You can relate to their stories and they may have ideas that will help your situation that you didn't think about. Your child needs support and so do you. In most communities, you can research local divorce support groups. Get yourself and your child into one as soon as possible.

MY NEW COMMITMENT:

The change I am making now is _____

I am committed to making this change by doing these 3 things differently:

1.

2.

3.

DO point out their strengths on a daily basis.

"I feel like I can accomplish goals and take risks. I know my mom and dad believe in me. Even when I don't do things right, they are sure to point out and tell me what strength I have and encourage me learn from my mistakes so I get stronger. Because they notice the strengths in me, I feel like I can take chances and go for my dreams." **Emily, age 16**

Every child has strengths. What are your children's gifts? Look for them in everyday interactions. Everything you tell them over and over again will help shape how they see themselves. The labels they carry in their mind end up making them the people they will become. Tell a child they are capable and you believe in their ability to figure it out, and they will become an adult who is able to problem solve. Tell a child they are an idiot, and they will become an adult who believes they can only work a minimum wage job for the rest of their life. You are their most important person in their life. Make sure the label you are imprinting in their mind is one of strength and self-confidence in them.

MY NEW COMMITMENT:

The change I am making now is _____

I am committed to making this change by doing these 3 things differently:

1.

2.

3.

> **DO find something going right, in the midst of everything appearing to go wrong, and talk about what is going right.**

"I can't seem to do anything right. I get 3 A's, a B and a C and all my parents focus on is the C. I have so much negative in my life, I just want to escape this all!" **Noah, age 17**

Perspective is everything. For example, a teen who is yelling at their mother can be labeled as a "disrespectful, ungrateful brat". A more positive perspective of that same situation can be framed as "a teen with a strong voice and passionate opinions who wants to communicate and be heard." However you view that teen will determine the outcome of your interaction. If you notice what is going right, then you will have the power to shape the conversation into a respectful, teachable moment. If you focus on what is going wrong, then the situation will quickly deteriorate into an emotionally draining, hurtful and frustrating experience. Avoid a power struggle. Notice what is going right (this takes some pause and thought), and then comment out loud on what it is you observe to be going right. This will soften the tone of every interaction. When you aren't heated and reactive, you create positive interactions. And, by the way, you will feel calmer AND you will start to "like" your child better, which is definitely a bonus. Say things such as:

"I noticed that you got your homework out and are working really hard. You are really responsible."

or

"Wow, you got such incredible grades. You clearly worked hard and achieved great goals. You must be so proud of yourself!"

MY NEW COMMITMENT:

The change I am making now is _____

I am committed to making this change by doing these 3 things differently:

1.

2.

3.

DO express your love, even in all their imperfections.

"I bumped my mom's favorite vase when I put my heavy backpack on the table. It fell over, broke and water spilled all over her papers. I waited for the big reaction. I saw her take a really deep breath, and after she sat in silence for a moment, she said, 'Well, let's get towels and I will help you clean it up. Accidents happen to everyone.' **Carley, age 9**

There is no better gift than unconditional acceptance. You can build self-worth in your child when you help them believe that they are truly accepted – *mistakes and all.* If you flip out when they make a mistake, or if you criticize and degrade them when they mess up, they will automatically take on the belief that they are "bad". When they feel they are bad, their self-worth diminishes. Help them understand that making a mistake isn't the same as being a mistake. If they fear messing up, they are less likely to take risks. If they believe that everyone messes up and they are still loved, worthy and accepted, then they will be more willing to take chances. In order to succeed in life, you need to be willing to risk making mistakes. The children that believe they are worthy, no matter what, will be better unafraid to try new things along with being better problem solvers.

MY NEW COMMITMENT:

The change I am making now is _____

I am committed to making this change by doing these 3 things differently:

1.

2.

3.

DO allow your children to hear you talk nicely about their other parent.

"I hate it when my dad says bad things about my mom. Even when he isn't saying anything really obviously awful, I can tell by the WAY he is saying it that he doesn't like her. I wish they wouldn't hate each other." **Mark, age 16**

Talk nicely about the other parent no matter how you feel. It shows respect, therefore, teaches respect. There is something positive you can say. If you talk badly about the other parent, then the truth is your children won't respect you. Take the high road. Find something you can offer as a compliment to the other parent. You will be the one they admire and respect when you do this.

MY NEW COMMITMENT:

The change I am making now is _____

I am committed to making this change by doing these 3 things differently:

1.

2.

3.

DO "good parenting" like you would do "good business."

"I feel good knowing that my parents tell me when I have appointments and keep me informed about what plans they have for me. I like that they pick me up when they say they will. I like knowing that even though they are divorced, I can still count on both of them." **Sara, age 10**

Decrease your child's anxiety by making sure you keep good ethics in place, just like you would practice good business. Make appointments in advance where both parents can plan to be present for the meeting, conference, doctor's visit, etc. Be on time and don't inconvenience the other parent. Respond right away to communications pertaining to your child. You decrease the worry within your child when you practice "good business" with the other parent.

MY NEW COMMITMENT:

The change I am making now is _____

I am committed to making this change by doing these 3 things differently:

1.

2.

3.

CHAPTER 3
RED FLAGS: DO SOMETHING!

Pay attention to these signs & symptoms that can result from divorce:

Irritability	Impulsive behaviors	Acting out
Dropping grades	Change in peer group	Using drugs
Defiance	Anger	Ditching School
Withdrawing from others	Isolating from friends	Testing rules and limits
Self-blame	Guilt and shame	Cutting/ Self-mutilation
Suicidal thoughts/ behaviors	Superficial positive behavior	Sneakiness
"Parenting" the needy parent	Overwhelmed	Detaching from home life
Rebellious	Sad more often	Sexually Active
Increased aggression	Destructive behaviors	Feelings of worthlessness
Drinking	Criminal acts	Failure to take responsibility
Increased manipulation	Confusion	Lying

If you notice a change in behavior, head them off at the pass. Minimize the negative impact of divorce. Face the reality of what is happening to fix the problem faster. DON'T WAIT until you are in an uncontrollable crisis. Call and seek help immediately when you first notice warning signs.

CHAPTER 4

YOU ARE ON YOUR WAY TO AN INCREDIBLE LIFE!

DIVORCE CHANGES A CHILD.

After a divorce, every phase of that child's life is forever changed. Every aspect of life is different now. They will experience childhood in a different way, their teen years in a changed way and their view of marriage will be seen through a completely different lens. Realizing their entire life has been altered, you can apply what you have learned to make a profound impact on their future.

YOU HAVE INCREDIBLE POWER.

You could have been that parent that chose to do nothing or bury your head in the sand, but you weren't. You decided to take the reins and move in a positive direction. Your devotion to parenting will produce an adult who can love and be loved, give and receive love and believe they are worthy of time, love and attention. Your investment in your children throughout your divorce will shape them to know, with every fiber of their being, that they are truly valuable, accepted, loved and whole. Your efforts will help them realize their strength, passion, gifts and capability to create a great life, no matter what has happened in their past.

Give yourself credit for what you DID learn and apply. Little by little, re-read and apply more of what you learned. Human brains can't take information and apply it perfectly the first time around. Celebrate what you have learned and KEEP coming back to reading this book and all the valuable things you have written in it. Watch how you evolve. You learn something new, you apply the information, then you repeat this over and over again. One year from now, you will be able to look back on all you wrote and be impressed and in awe of how far you have come. You will have grown, changed, and transformed your life and your child's future because of the choices you have made today. Congratulations!

LETTER FROM THE AUTHOR...

It is with great, tender care that I have written this book – I am dedicated to this process of helping families because I care. I know the pains of divorce. I also know healing from the brokenness. I admire your strength and courage to take on the challenge of being the best person and parent you can be. Parenting is the hardest job in the world, but the payoffs are priceless. The process of change is a very difficult, amazing and powerful process. You and your child are worth every ounce of investment and effort you devote to your family. You can't necessarily control everything about the divorce process, but as mothers and fathers of your children, you certainly can enrich the process so that your children come out happy and healthy on the other end. I wish you the very best life has to offer and for always, I wish you HOPE, HEALING & HAPPINESS!

Fondly,
     Dilyse

P.S. I would love to hear your personal stories and how this book affected your life. Write to me at Dilyse@DilyseDiazTherapy.com

www.ingramcontent.com/pod-product-compliance
Lightning Source LLC
Chambersburg PA
CBHW072210090426
42740CB00012B/2462